tourism TATTLER

Issue 02 (FEBRUARY) 2016

PUBLISHER
Tourism Tattler (Pty) Ltd.
PO Box 891, Umhlanga Rocks, 4320
KwaZulu-Natal, South Africa.
Website: www.tourismtattler.com

EXECUTIVE EDITOR Des Langkilde
Cell: +27 (0)82 374 7260
Fax: +27 (0)86 651 8080
E-mail: editor@tourismtattler.com
Skype: tourismtattler

MAGAZINE ADVERTISING
ADVERTISING DIRECTOR Bev Langkilde
Cell: +27 (0)71 224 9971
Fax: +27 (0)86 656 3860
E-mail: bev@tourismtattler.com
Skype: bevtourismtattler

SUBSCRIPTIONS
http://eepurl.com/bocIdD

BACK ISSUES (Click on the covers below).

▼ JAN 2016 ▼ Dec 2015 ▼ Nov 2015
▼ Oct 2015 ▼ Sep 2015 ▼ Aug 2015
▼ Jul 2015 ▼ Jun 2015 ▼ May 2015
▼ Apr 2015 ▼ Mar 2015 ▼ Feb 2015

Contents

I0494515

10 BUSINESS: Travel Trade Challenges in 2016.

16 EVENTS: 14 Amazing African Festivals for 2016.

30 TRANSPORT: Mercedes-Benz Sprinter sets the standard for vans.

IN THIS ISSUE

EDITORIAL CONTRIBUTORS

Adv. Louis Nel
Claire Allison

Dr. Peter E. Tarlow
Kagiso Mosue

Martin Janse van Vuuren
Prof Melville Saayman

MAGAZINE SPONSORS

Add Fancourt to your Conference Bucket List

FANCOURT
SOUTH AFRICA

ONLY 7KM FROM GEORGE AIRPORT, WITH DAILY FLIGHTS FROM MAJOR CITIES, DELEGATES CAN CHOOSE FROM 115 FANCOURT HOTEL ROOMS AND 18 MANOR HOUSE SUITES AND AN ASSORTMENT OF LEISURE ACTIVITIES – GIVING BUSINESS TRAVELLERS MORE THAN SIMPLY CONFERENCING AND BANQUETING.

MEETINGS, INCENTIVES, CONFERENCES & EVENTS

- Fully equipped conference centre, meeting and events venue
- Large multi-purpose ballroom on the upper floor
- Six meeting rooms situated on the upper levels
- Spacious foyers on two levels
- Capacity from small groups to 400
- All meeting rooms have natural daylight
- On-site technician and IT support

WINTER AT FANCOURT – THE PERFECT TIME

- Underfloor heating and heated towel rails
- Warm scented and personalised towels
- Luxury hot chocolate and marshmallow turndowns
- Heated indoor pool, gym and instruction studio
- Heated therapeutic Roman Bath and Luxury Spa
- Wood-fired pizza venue with complimentary Glühwein
- No rumbling tummies with our 5 star hot breakfast buffet!

Terms and conditions apply
Group Reservations 044 804 0020 or groupreservations@fancourt.co.za
www.fancourt.com

BOOKING CODE: 16GCWTT

THE LEADING HOTELS OF THE WORLD®

BOKAY DESIGNS

078 894 1811 • info@bokaydesigns.co.za • www.bokaydesigns.co.za

PLUGINS DIGITAL DESIGN **GRAPHIC** & SOCIAL CMS
LAYOUT **BRANDING** SEO RESPONSIVE
COLOUR FONTS **WEB** HTML5
CUSTOMER CODING CSS **WORDPRESS** DESIGN
IMAGE VISUAL **DESIGN** LAYOUT
CREATIVE

As a freelance designer I strive to combine simplicity with technical functionality in digital, social and print communications.

WEBSITE DESIGN

I leverage the powerful WordPress publishing platform to build awesome, mobile responsive websites that rank well and are easy for clients to manage.

GRAPHIC DESIGN

I develop creative ideas and concepts, choosing the appropriate media and style to meet my client's objectives. Projects are undertaken from start to finished product.

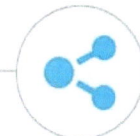

SOCIAL MEDIA

I can help you with set-up and/or daily monitoring and posts for your business to grow your social influence and generate sales leads.

Save **10% off** your first project! 078 894 1811

Accreditation

The Africa Travel Association (ATA)

Tel: +1 212 447 1357 • Email: _info@africatravelassociation.org_ • Website: _www.africatravelassociation.org_

ATA is a division of the Corporate Council on Africa (CCA), and a registered non-profit trade association in the USA, with headquarters in Washington, DC and chapters around the world. ATA is dedicated to promoting travel and tourism to Africa and strengthening intra-Africa partnerships. Established in 1975, ATA provides services to both the public and private sectors of the industry.

The African Travel & Tourism Association (Atta)

Tel: +44 20 7937 4408 • Email: _info@atta.travel_ • Website: _www.atta.travel_

Members in 22 African countries and 37 worldwide use Atta to: Network and collaborate with peers in African tourism; Grow their online presence with a branded profile; Ask and answer specialist questions and give advice; and Attend key industry events.

National Accommodation Association of South Africa (NAA-SA)

Tel: +2786 186 2272 • Fax: +2786 225 9858 • Website: _www.naa-sa.co.za_

The NAA-SA is a network of mainly smaller accommodation providers around South Africa – from B&Bs in country towns offering comfortable personal service to luxurious boutique city lodges with those extra special touches – you're sure to find a suitable place, and at the same time feel confident that your stay at an NAA-SA member's establishment will meet your requirements.

Regional Tourism Organisation of Southern Africa (RETOSA)

Tel: +2711 315 2420/1 • Fax: +2711 315 2422 • Website: _www.retosa.co.za_

RETOSA is a Southern African Development Community (SADC) institution responsible for tourism growth and development. RETOSA's aims are to increase tourist arrivals to the region through. RETOSA Member States are Angola, Botswana, DR Congo, Lesotho, Madagascar, Malawi, Mauritius, Mozambique, Namibia, Seychelles, South Africa, Swaziland, Tanzania, Zambia and Zimbabwe.

Southern Africa Tourism Services Association (SATSA)

Tel: +2786 127 2872 • Fax: +2711 886 755 • Website: _www.satsa.com_

SATSA is a credibility accreditation body representing the private sector of the inbound tourism industry. SATSA members are Bonded thus providing a financial guarantee against advance deposits held in the event of the involuntary liquidation. SATSA represents: Transport providers, Tour Operators, DMC's, Accommodation Suppliers, Tour Brokers, Adventure Tourism Providers, Business Tourism Providers and Allied Tourism Services providers.

Southern African Vehicle Rental and Leasing Association (SAVRALA)

Contact: _manager@savrala.co.za_ • Website: _w_

Founded in the 1970's, SAVRALA is the representative voice of Southern Africa's vehicle rental, leasing and fleet management sector. Our members have a combined national footprint with more than 600 branches countrywide. SAVRALA are instrumental in steering industry standards and continuously strive to protect both their members' interests, and those of the public, and are therefore widely respected within corporate and government sectors.

Seychelles Hospitality & Tourism Association (SHTA)

Tel: +248 432 5560 • Fax: +248 422 5718 • Website: _www.shta.sc_

The Seychelles Hospitality and Tourism Association was created in 2002 when the Seychelles Hotel Association merged with the Seychelles Hotel and Guesthouse Association. SHTA's primary focus is to unite all Seychelles tourism industry stakeholders under one association in order to be better prepared to defend the interest of the industry and its sustainability as the pillar of the country's economy.

International Coalition of Tourism Partners (ICTP)

Website: _www.tourismpartners.org_

ICTP is a travel and tourism coalition of global destinations committed to Quality Services and Green Growth.

International Institute for Peace through Tourism

Website: _www.iipt.org_

IIPT is dedicated to fostering tourism initiatives that contribute to international understanding and cooperation.

World Travel Market

WTM Africa - Cape Town in April, _WTM Latin America_ - São Paulo in April, and _WTM - London_ in November. WTM is the place to do business.

World Youth Student and Educational (WYSE) Travel Confederation

Website: _www.wysetc.org_

WYSE is a global not-for-profit membership organisation.

The Safari Awards

Website: _www.safariawards.com_

Safari Award finalists are amongst the top 3% in Africa and the winners are unquestionably the best.

World Luxury Hotel Awards

Website: _www.luxuryhotelawards.com_

World Luxury Hotel Awards is an international company that provides award recognition to the best hotels from all over the world.

INSPIRING SPIER EXPERIENCES

Spier is one of the oldest wine farms in South Africa with a recorded history dating back to 1692. While rooted in this heritage, Spier has a vibrant and conscious energy. Award-winning wine can be paired with fabulous food, grown either on the farm or by nearby farmers. The winery is one of the most awarded in the country and the four-star Spier Hotel and meeting facilities offer inspiring Winelands getaways in the tranquillity of nature.

Spier is not just a great destination, however. Our passion for quality and sustainability touches everything we do. We constantly strive to find innovative ways for our business to succeed in balance with our environment and society.

ACCOMMODATION

Spier Hotel is situated alongside the banks of the calming Eerste River and features 153 rooms clustered around tranquil courtyards.

CONSCIOUS CONFERENCING

From the conference centre (which includes a 450-seat auditorium), to the historic Manor House, Spier can cater for large and small conferences, seminars, launches and exhibitions.

WINE

A comprehensive selection of Spier's award- winning vintages (paired with delicious food) can be sampled at our tasting room on the banks of Spier dam. The wine is available for purchase at cellar door prices.

EXPLORING

Take a tour on a Segway and learn about the way we farm and Spier's wastewater recycling plant. Stroll past historic buildings, explore the beautiful reclaimed Werf or amongst indigenous flowers on our Protea Walk.

CONTACT DETAILS: + 27 21 809 1100   reservations@spier.co.za   www.spier.co.za   f www.facebook.com/spierwinefarm   🐦 @SpierWineFarm

Tour Operator App to Boost Rural Tourism

An innovative online product aims to assist tour operators in sourcing new, emerging and community-based tourism businesses and experiences for their tours and itineraries, writes **Claire Allison**.

Local non-profit organisation Open Africa in partnership with Die Deutsche Gesellschaft für Internationale Zusammenarbeit (GIZ) are working together on innovative project to develop an online product that will assist tour operators with the process of sourcing new, emerging and community-based tourism businesses and experiences for their tours and itineraries.

The project aims to provide local tour operators with a wider range and better product knowledge of the emerging and community-based tourism segment which is hoped will increase businesses between emerging and community-based enterprises and established tour operators.

The partnership comes after Open Africa, together with the Responsible & Inclusive Business Hub (RIBH) from GIZ, hosted a networking session in August 2015 with selected tour operators to explore the challenges faced by including community-based tourism enterprises in their itineraries and to see how those challenges could be overcome. The workshop provided valuable insight into the business practices of tour operators and a number of innovative ideas were discussed.

Open Africa will also develop a toolkit with practical resources to assist tourism enterprises to deliver a high-quality hospitality experience. This will be tailored to the type of business as these range from attractions to accommodation, activities and tour guides.

The tool will also allow tour operators to assess, score and provide feedback to attractions, accommodation and tour guides that participate in the programme. The product will be launched in May 2016 at the annual Tourism Indaba in Durban, where tour operators will be given a live illustration of the product features.

It is hoped that the product will increase understanding on the part of emerging and community-based tourism enterprises of the needs and requirements of tour operators and how they can improve their businesses to meet these standards consistently. In return, tour operators will have more trust in the ability of these establishments and will be more likely to include them on future itineraries.

Open Africa Managing Director, Francois Viljoen said, "the project is exciting since it provides both tour operators and community-based enterprises practical tools to build stronger linkages and will

ultimately improve the quality of experiences provided in the industry. By exposing tour operators to new products and helping to bridge the gap and create market access for the emerging entrepreneurs, rural economies in South Africa can be sustained and expect growth through job creation, new income streams and increased awareness of tourism offerings.

Open Africa is a social enterprise that helps rural entrepreneurs feel confident to work together to revitalise their communities through tourism. It opens people's eyes to the untapped potential of areas outside of the city, and helps them overcome the obstacles to growth. Open Africa has worked with communities to establish 64 branded tourism routes throughout 6 countries in Southern Africa over the past 20 years.

About the author: Claire Allison is the marketing manager of Open Africa. www.openafrica.org

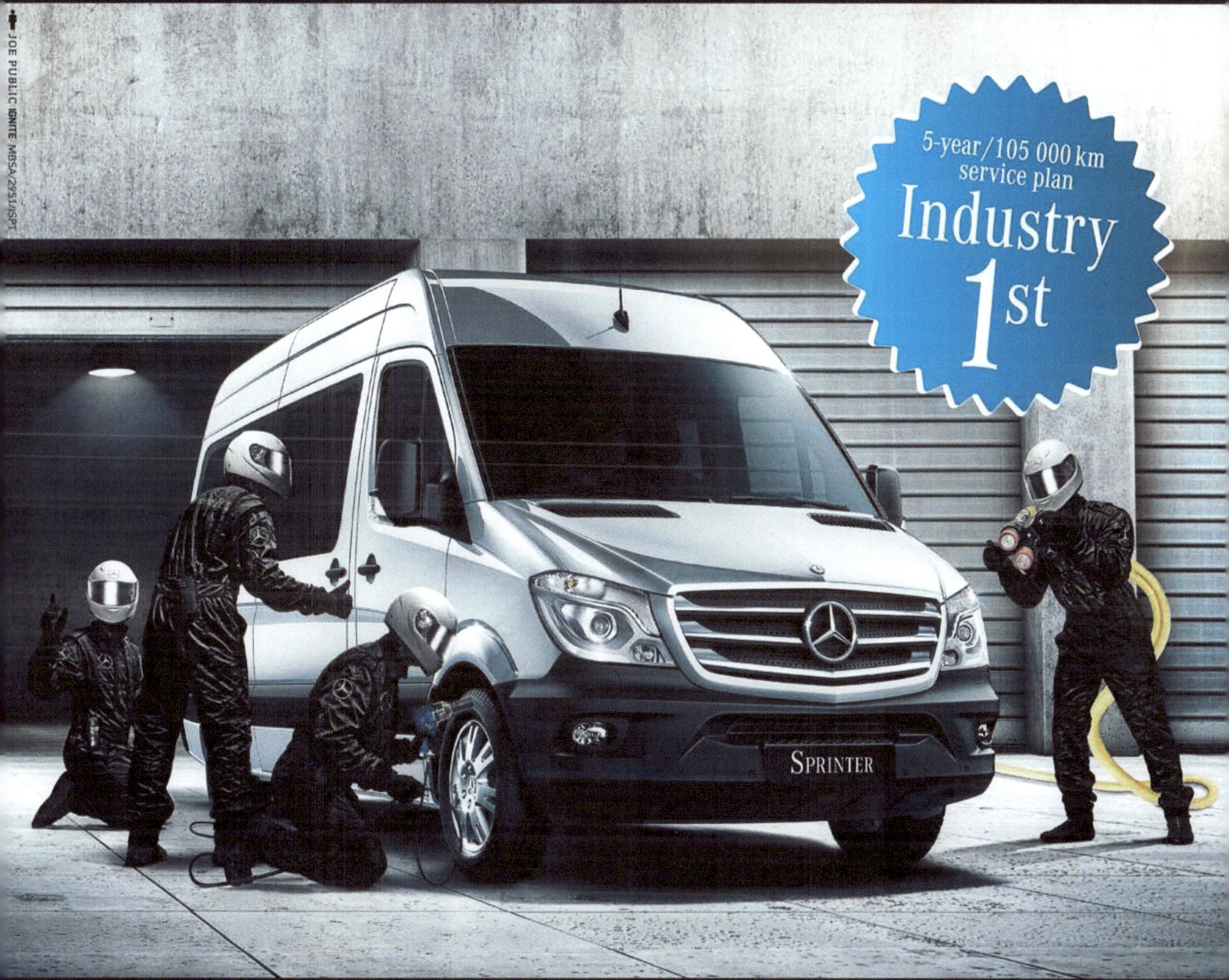

SATSA
Southern Africa Tourism Services Association
BONDED*

Market Intelligence Report

Grant Thornton

The information below was extracted from data available as at **01 February 2016**. By **Martin Jansen van Vuuren** of **Grant Thornton**.

ARRIVALS

The latest available data from **Statistics South Africa** is for **January to November 2015***:

	Current period	Change over same period last year
UK	352 878	-0.4%
Germany	229 252	-7.3%
USA	268 535	-5.1%
India	72 031	-9.3%
China (incl Hong Kong)	76 888	-3.4%
Overseas Arrivals	1 910 465	-6.0%
African Arrivals	6 088 827	-7.3%
Total Foreign Arrivals	8 011 053	-7.0%

HOTEL STATS

The latest available data from **STR Global** is for **January** to **December 2015**:

Current period	Average Room Occupancy (ARO)	Average Room Rate (ARR)	Revenue Per Available Room (RevPAR)
All Hotels in SA	63.4%	R 1 086	R 688
All 5-star hotels in SA	63.0%	R 1 981	R 1 249
All 4-star hotels in SA	62.6%	R 1 024	R 641
All 3-star hotels in SA	63.4%	R 871	R 552
Change over same period last year			
All Hotels in SA	1.4%	6.5%	8.0%
All 5-star hotels in SA	1.3%	9.5%	11.0%
All 4-star hotels in SA	2.2%	5.3%	7.6%
All 3-star hotels in SA	-0.2%	6.2%	5.9%

ACSA DATA

The latest available data from **ACSA** is for **January** to **December 2015**:

Change over same period last year	Passengers arriving on International Flights	Passengers arriving on Regional Flights	Passengers arriving on Domestic Flights
OR Tambo International	0.3%	-1.8%	10.1%
Cape Town International	8.9%	11.0%	8.8%
King Shaka International	-4.7%	N/A	7.3%

CAR RENTAL DATA

The latest available data from **SAVRALA** is for **January to June 2015**:

	Current period	Change over same period last year
Industry rental days	8 139 127	-1%
Industry utilisation	70.2%	-0.7%
Industry Average daily revenue	2 498 944 728	1%

WHAT THIS MEANS FOR MY BUSINESS

Analyses of Statistics South Africa data shows that foreign arrivals are at 2013 levels. The tourism industry in South Africa is currently being propped up by domestic tourism. It is hoped that the depreciation of the Rand coupled with the implementation of the revised visa regulations will lead to a recovery in the growth of foreign arrivals. *Note that African Arrivals plus Overseas Arrivals do not add to Total Foreign Arrivals due to the exclusion of unspecified arrivals, which could not be allocated to either African or Overseas. As from January 2014, Stats SA has stopped counting people transiting through SA as tourists. As a result of the revision, in order to compare the 2014 figures with 2013, it is necessary to deduct the transit figures from the 2013 totals.*

For more information contact Martin at Grant Thornton on +27 (0)12 417 8838 or visit: http://www.gt.co.za

South Africa

Strong Domestic Leisure Demand Lifts Q4 2015 Business Performance

Strong domestic leisure demand has helped to lift South Africa's travel and tourism business performance in the last quarter of 2015, writes **Kagiso Mosue.**

The Tourism Business Index (TBI) report for Q4 2015 released by the Tourism Business Council of South Africa (TBCSA) shows that overall, the industry achieved above normal business performance levels, recording a TBI score of 106.5* compared to the anticipated but more subdued TBI score of 94.2. This is the only quarter in 2015 to achieve above normal business performance levels and the third highest recorded Q4 index since 2011.

Business performance outlook for the first quarter of 2016 is slightly below normal levels, reaching a TBI score of 94.6.

In terms of inbound tourism, both the Accommodation Sector and the 'Other Tourism Businesses' segment (excluding accommodation) cited the weak exchange rate as the most prominent positive factor stimulating foreign tourism leisure demand. However, domestic tourism leisure demand proved to be the biggest performance driver over this period.

"The festive season is typically one of our busiest times, presenting the trade with the opportunity to do some good business when many people, particularly locals, take some time off to travel. After a tough three quarters of trade, we've been anxiously looking towards to the festive period for some welcomed reprieve in the market," said TBCSA Chief Executive Officer, Ms. Mmatšatši Ramawela.

Recent tourism statistics from provinces such as KwaZulu-Natal and the Western Cape suggest that the outlying coastal areas were the most popular tourism spots visited. "The weak exchange rate certainly made destination South Africa a lot more attractive to foreign tourists, but we must also keep in mind that it also made it a lot more affordable for South Africans to travel locally, hence the increase in domestic tourism demand " Ramawela explains.

Other positive contributing factors cited for the improvement in tourism business performance in Q4 include a decrease in supply due to the closure of several establishments, new management in the value chain, an increase in marketing activities and improvements in customer service, flexibility and staff training.

Although the cited decline in supply is a positive outcome from a competitor point of view, Ramawela cautions that if this trend continues, it will reveal an overall contraction of supply, which is not a good sign for the industry. "Closures can be attributed to businesses being under tremendous pressure.

More and more of them are finding it hard to compete in the current environment that is largely characterised by rising cost of inputs, lacklustre business and leisure demand as well as uncertainty in government policies affecting the industry. As one of the few sectors that have a great potential to boost economic growth in the country, we simply must do more to ensure that this trend does not continue".

When it comes to overall business performance outlook for the new year, business expectation is mixed. A large percentage of the Accommodation Sector (51%) anticipate business performance levels to remain the same, whilst a large portion of Other Tourism Businesses (44%) is expecting to achieve better than normal business performance (despite their pessimistic outlook for Q1).

Grant Thornton's Head of Advisory Services, Ms Gillian Saunders, explained that given the dynamics in the operating environment and uncertainty in many business arenas, it is not easy to predict performance levels for the rest of the year, hence the differences in opinion on overall outlook.

Marc Corcoran, President of the Southern African Vehicle Rental and Leasing Association (SAVRALA) added that from a car rental perspective, even though overall performance over the festive season was good, the industry faces a difficult operating climate in 2016 as the Rand's depreciation will impact on new vehicle pricing which is a critical cost driver in the car rental industry, inevitably resulting in higher rental rates".

For this quarter, the index survey included additional questions on the impact of concessions announced by the Cabinet Inter-Ministerial Committee on Immigration. Respondents were asked about the impact of the revisions on the requirement for foreign visitors travelling with children to carry unabridged birth certificates. Almost half, 48.4%, of the respondents cite that there was no impact from the original requirements (i.e. not applicable), whilst 16.4% have seen a partial reversal of the previous negative impact as a result of the changes and 13.2% have continued to experience a strong negative impact regardless of the changes.

Similarly, respondents were asked about the impact of the planned implementation of biometric data capturing by the Department of Home Affairs. 62.2% of respondents were not affected by the introduction of the regulation (i.e. considered not applicable to their establishment), whilst 26.9% of respondents still feel the negative impact despite the move, and 10.9% noted a reversal of the previous negative impact.

"Even as we begin a new year, issues related to visa regulations and the broad issue of travel facilitation remains top of mind for us" Ramawela said. "So far, the figures are showing that the impact of the concessions announced have not had such a significant effect. We eagerly look forward to the announcement by the Department of Home Affairs regarding their work of implementing the concessions announced at the end of October 2015 by the Cabinet Inter-Ministerial Committee. Furthermore, we look forward to our engagement with the Departments of Home Affairs and Tourism and the local and international trade to work together to ensure that South Africa regains its market share of international and regional tourist arrivals."

* An index score of 100 indicates normal levels of acceptable business performance. When the index shows performance or prospects higher than 100, this indicates better than normal performance, whilst below 100 indicates worse than normal performance

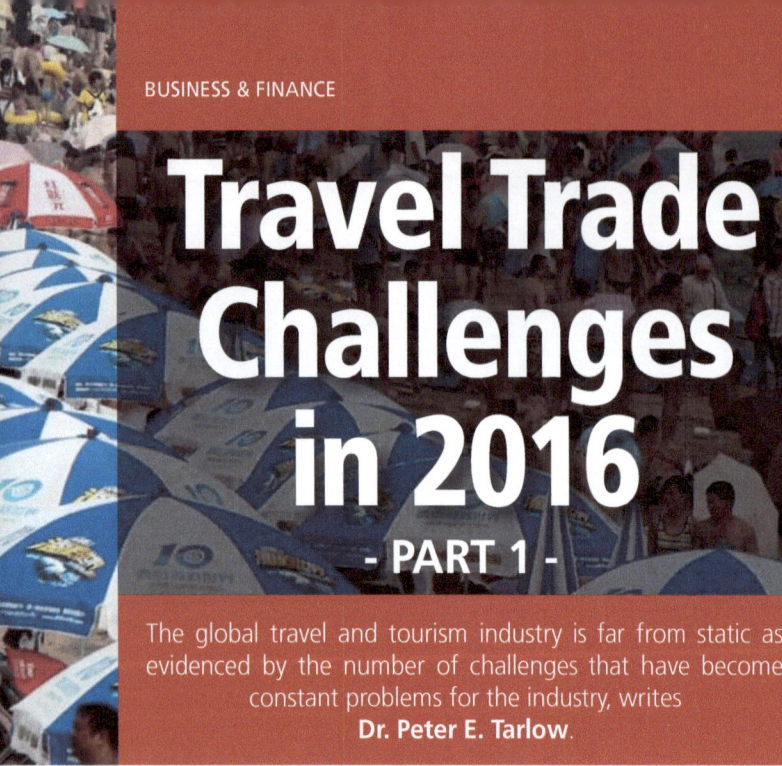

Travel Trade Challenges in 2016
- PART 1 -

The global travel and tourism industry is far from static as evidenced by the number of challenges that have become constant problems for the industry, writes **Dr. Peter E. Tarlow**.

The recent stock market ups and downs are a real indication of the turbulence that may impact tourism in 2016 and present new challenges to tourism professionals around the world.

Here are some of the challenges and a few suggestions on how to overcome them:

High Taxation on the Tourism Industry

There is a mistaken belief that visitors and tourists do not pay taxes. Nothing could be further from the truth. Instead tourists are some of the highest taxed and under represented people in the world. We only have to examine an airline ticket, rent a car, or stay at a hotel to realise how much we spend on travel.

These taxes not only add a great deal to the cost of travel, but they have also become nuisances. For example, departing from many places requires an exit payment, and in all too many other locations visas are nothing more than an additional way to victimise tourists. Because tourists are generally not citizens of the places that they visit, they have no political voice. However, the local members of the tourism industry can act as their voice. Tourism, as with any other product, has an economic saturation limit and if taxes become overly burdensome local tourism businesses will see a reduction in their profits.

Increase of mass tourism resulting in straining tourism infrastructure

Many places around the world have seen large numbers of tourist arrivals but are simply not prepared to handle the influx. Tourism is much more than merely selling or marketing. There has to be a product and the product must be composed not only of the attraction or activity, but also the personnel who deliver the product. This means that if the number of visitors is greater than the capacity of a location to absorb these visitors, the locale will suffer numerous problems.

Often too many visitors to a destination that is ill prepared for non-sustainable numbers creates a sense of tourism euphoria in the short term, but introduces long term tourism problems that may become deadly to the sustained health of a tourism industry. An easy check to see if a particular tourism product's infrastructure is over extended is to determine the percentage of visitors who wish to return. If few visitors desire to return, then this may be an indication that the price-tourism structure continuum is reaching unsustainable limits.

Airports not adept for modern tourism

Perhaps the biggest problem exists in the realm of airports. Many airports are simply not equipped to handle a large number of passengers arriving at the same time. This lack of infrastructure combined with often poorly trained personnel (or personnel who simply do not care) creates long lines and unpleasant memories. Tourism officials need to remember that first and last impressions are key components in their marketing efforts.

Local Infrastructure problems

Too many tourism destinations are not prepared for tourists. They lack good sanitation facilities and water treatment plants. Likewise both roads and sidewalks are not well maintained, creating hazards not only for the local population but also for the visitor population. It is essential that local governments take into consideration that a good tourism environment also impacts the local culture and environment. Heavy taxes with poor road and street quality are sure not only to upset citizens but are a warning sign that tourism may be headed toward future problems.

Customer service is key to a healthy tourism industry

The least expensive and most important part of the tourism experience is customer–visitor interaction. Smiles and a friendly handshake or nod of the head cost nothing and can change a negative impression into a positive one. Unfortunately tourism personnel often forget that the visitor is their employer and that when visitations cease so do their jobs. Too many people who work in tourism are civil servants who cannot be fired. Job protection needs to be a reward and not a right. When there are no consequences for bad behaviour or rudeness on the part of tourism personnel, not only is the product's reputation diminished but so too is the quality of the tourism offering.

Providing quality customer service is an ongoing challenge for many parts of the tourism industry. Although it is the least expensive challenge to face, it has proven to be one of the hardest challenges to meet and overcome.

Below are some suggestions to help face these problems.

Develop a tourism vision

You cannot begin to create infrastructure if you do not know what form of tourism your locale desires. Not every form of tourism is correct for every locale, and no locale can be all things to all people. Think through what forms of tourism best meet your community's needs and how tourism will add to the quality of life for your community. Once you have the vision of what type of tourism you desire, you can then begin to analyse if the vision is realistic and obtainable, and finally what obstacles stand in the way of creating this vision

Bundle taxes

Most tourism entities cannot control what governments choose to do when it comes to taxation, but the industry is not powerless.

Do everything possible to ease the taxation burden and to make payments as easy as possible. For example, include airport, bus station or seaport entrance and exit fees in the cost of a ticket. Forcing visitors to go from one line to the next in order to depart wins the local tourism industry few friends and creates a negative final image of the locale.

Simplify currency exchange laws and procedures

Tourism can produce a great deal of hard currency for any particular location. However, when exchange centres such as banks and hotels overcharge for the purchase of local currency, there is a tendency to go to the black market, not to respect local laws, or put oneself in danger. Post rates of exchange and where currency can be exchanged legally and at what times. Post prices whenever possible in both the local currency and in an international currency such as dollars or euros, and Chinese yuan.

Seek out-of-the-box solutions

The bottom line is that no matter what the problem may be do not give up. Be creative, smile and remember that tourism is all about turning challenges into new and exciting opportunities. Find new partners, for example seek the aid of law enforcement, the local school boards, or hospitals to create new solutions to old problems.

Part 2 will be published in the March edition.

About the Author: Dr. Peter E. Tarlow *publishes a monthly 'Tourism Tidbits' newsletter. He is a founder of the Texas chapter of TTRA, President of T&M, and a popular author and speaker on tourism. Tarlow is a specialist in the areas of sociology of tourism, economic development, tourism safety and security. Tarlow speaks at governors' and state conferences on tourism and conducts seminars throughout the world. For more information e-mail ptarlow@tourismandmore.com*

Competition

The winning 'Like' or 'Share' during the month of **February 2016** will receive a
set of 5 Stonecast crockery pots with the compliments of **Livingstones Supply Co** – *Suppliers of the Finest Products to the Hospitality Industry*.

'Like' / 'Share' / 'Connect' with these Social Media icons to win!

Livingston Supply Company

Tourism Tattler

Competition Rules: Only one winner will be selected each month on a random selection draw basis. The prize winner will be notified via social media. The prize will be delivered by the sponsor to the winners postal address within South Africa. Should the winner reside outside of South Africa, delivery charges may be applicable. The prize may not be exchanged for cash.

The Stonecast crockery pots are available in Paprika or Pebble colours, and the set of 5 pots includes:
1x Dipper pot 5.5 x 5.8cm
1x Dipper pot 6.7 x 6.9cm
1x Dip Dish 3.5 x 9.7cm
1x Chip pot 9 x9.7cm

Congratulations to our January Social Media winner

@Botha_JP6w

Johannes Botha has been selected as our **January 2016** winner for his 'Follow & Tweet' on **Twitter.**
Johannes will receive a **6-cup (800ml) Chrome Coffee Maker** with the compliments of **Livingstones Supply Co** – *Suppliers of the Finest Products to the Hospitality Industry.*

For more information visit www.livingstonessupplyco.com

Meerkat Adventures

A meerkat conservation project established in 2008 to educate both farmers and tourists alike on the need for protection of these shy suricate's has developed into a unique tourist attraction and South Africa's first meerkat sanctuary, writes **Des Langkilde.**

I met Devey Glinister while doing a property review on De Zeekoe guest farm in Oudtshoorn *(see page 21)* after joining a tour group for a meerkat experience on the farm at sunrise.

Witnessing a clan of meerkat in the wild as they go about their daily routine would have been impossible due to their shy and elusive nature, were it not for Devey's patience and perseverance in habituating this particular clan to the presence of humans over many years. Meerkats are part of the so-called 'Shy 5' which includes the bat-eared fox, the aardvark, porcupine and aardwolf.

The meerkat tour is well organised and includes coffee and rusks at a bush site, which forms part of De Zeekoe farm just off the R62 about seven kilometres from Oudtshoorn. Lightweight folding chairs are handed out to each guest as dawn approaches and the group are then lead a short distance away to the nearest meerkat burrow, where everyone settles down with their backs to the East and the pending sunrise.

As the sun breaches the horizon, the dominant female is the first to scurry out of the burrow, and after checking the terrain for threats she gives an all-clear signal to the rest of the gang who slowly arise from the burrow, yawning and stretching. Ignoring the group of human onlookers, the gang shuffle for space and all face the sun with stomachs bared to warm up.

Davey tells us that this is their 'solar panel battery recharge' routine, and that the gang won't move off until they have all warmed up sufficiently. While the group of onlookers shutter away with their cameras, Davey educates us on the meerkats habits and why meerkat should not be kept as pets, while one of his team takes photos of the tour group, which are later emailed to each guest.

After about half an hour of watching the meerkat grooming each other and the young playing, we folded our chairs and followed the gang as they set off to forage, and noticed how one meerkat would always be on sentry duty by positioning itself on a mound of sand, a shrub or a bush to keep a lookout for threats.

At the end of the tour, which took around three hours, I asked Davey what he hoped to achieve with the meerkat conservation project.

"Firstly we would like to build a meerkat sanctuary for all the meerkat orphans that were previously kept as pets and cannot be set free again. We hope with the right research in the right environment we'll be able to rehabilitate and release. Secondly we would like to convert more landowners to make space on their farms for meerkats to live in their natural habitat," said Devey.

For more information visit www.meerkatadventures.co.za or email deveyg@gmail.com.

4 Big Ideas 4

● ● ● ● ● ● ● ● ● ●

Small Meetings

Getting big ideas from your corporate leadership team at strategy meetings is enhanced when the meeting is held at a venue away from the work environment.

Here are four big ideas for a venue and post-meeting activities that are sure to get the creative juices of your leadership team flowing (for up to 12 executives):

1. VENUE

The Manor House at Spier Wine Farm is a mere 24 minute (26 km) drive from Cape Town International Airport, and Spier's airport shuttle service can even collect your team on arrival. Located within The Manor House, the **De Clerque Room** boardroom table seats 12 people in style and comfort, and the plush Victorian era furnishings and ambiance are not detracted from by the modern business presentation equipment, which is discreetly tucked away in hidden recesses. Meeting in a room that has almost 300 years of heritage is sure to stimulate creative ideas.

2. REFRESHMENT BREAKS

Tea breaks are convened in the superbly decorated **Van Liewvens Lounge**, within the Manor House. Here, your executive team can enthusiastically discuss the morning or afternoon meeting sessions under original pieces of art, which form part of the Spier Arts Academy.

3. LUNCH

Active minds need nourishment, and Spier's delectable menu of wholesome farm grown food is purposely designed to enhance mental vitality. Lunch and dinner can be served in the **Reynholds Room** at the Manor House or at any one of three restaurants situated on the farm, namely Eight Restaurant, the Hotel Restaurant or the Hoghouse Bakery & Cafe. Alternately, your team could opt for a supplied picnic, selecting food and beverages, including Spier's famous wine selection, from the Eight To Go Deli.

4. SUNDOWNERS, SPA or TOUR

Wrap up your meeting with a glass Spier's award winning wine while admiring a spectacular African dusk overlooking the Spier dam with the Helderberg mountains as a backdrop. Or treat your mentally drained execs to a rejuvenating massage at the boutique Spier Hotel Spa followed, or preceded by a Segway or Eagle Encounters tour.

And finally, if your meeting concludes on a Friday why not check-in to the hotel and allow your executive team to relax over the weekend – perhaps with partners included.

For a tailor-made small meeting package contact Angela Lorimer on +27 (0) 809 1100 Ext 1 or email conference@spier.co.za

Status of Festivals in South Africa

Recent research into the status of festivals in South Africa has produced some interesting findings, writes **Prof Melville Snyman.**

Image: AfrikaBurn Festival 2013

The TREES (Tourism Research in Economic Environs and Society) research focus area at the North-West University, wanted to determine how many festivals there are and what types of festivals are hosted in each of South Africa's provinces.

Festivals have several benefits, which is one of the key reasons why regions want to host them, such as addressing seasonality, growing visitation numbers, promoting a town, region or destination, establishing an image, contributing to job creation, and providing locals the opportunity to experience something that they might otherwise never had the opportunity to experience.

These are just a few of the benefits. However, let us start by defining what a festival is – a festival is an event celebrating a unique aspect of a particular community and can be once-off or reoccurring. Therefore, one gets a variety of festivals such as arts, music, agricultural, wine, food, and religious, to name but a few, which are generally unique to a region or destination.

How was this research conducted?

First of all, we determined the number of festivals to create a database. Then we contacted the festival organisers who had to complete a questionnaire. One-hundred-and-fifty (150) festival organisers participated in the survey, and the results were interesting. First of all, the number of festivals in South Africa has increased significantly from approximately 100 in 1994 to 626 in 2015.

What are the top three types of festivals hosted in South Africa?

Results show these are arts (22%), food (16%) and wine (12%). These categories are based on the primary focus of the festival. Another 12% indicated that they combine several themes instead of focusing on just one. The average length of festivals is three days and most festivals (97%) are held annually.

If one looks at the distribution of festivals in South Africa, it reveals some very interesting facts and it is here that government can play a more proactive role in order to distribute festivals to a larger population in South Africa.

The province that hosts the most festivals is the Western Cape (46%), followed by Gauteng (18%) and the Eastern Cape (9%). If one looks at the different provinces and what they offer tourists or can offer tourists or *festinos*, it is clear that most provinces (cities or towns)

Festival Research Findings

Growth:
1994 = 100
2015 = 626.

Themes:
Arts = 22%
Food = 16%
Wine = 12%
Combined = 12%
Uncategorised = 38%.

Duration:
3 days.

Frequency:
97% annually.

Top provinces:
Western Cape = 46%
Gauteng = 18%
Eastern Cape = 9%.

Organiser Sentiment::
Static / Growth = 76%
Decline = 18%.

---

are not using festivals effectively in order to grow their visitation numbers and this is a huge missed opportunity. I am, however, not advocating more festivals for the sake of festivals, but rather more festivals that support what a city (community), town or region is all about. Festivals should therefore be unique to a region or city and most festivals start small, like any business opportunity, and then grow. Many festival organisers are discouraged if they do not attract thousands of visitors in year one.

One of the greatest advantages of festivals is that it also supports numerous entrepreneurs by giving them the opportunity to host events or market and sell their products. These entrepreneurs are also called *artrepreneurs* or *eventrepreneurs*. Festivals are therefore also a boost for the creative industries and if South Africa is serious about growing entrepreneurs and job creation, then we need to develop a strategy on how to grow this segment. The last and probably the most important question is:

Have festival organisers experienced a decline in attendance numbers?

With the significant increase in number of festivals, 18% of the respondents indicated that there is a decline; however, seventy-six percent (76%) indicated that they have not experienced declines. Festivals are dependent on sponsorships, and getting the local community involved in hosting the festival is important.

Festivals are an important part of the tourism offering, and some of the festivals in South Africa are internationally renown. South Africa has an opportunity to position more festivals on the international calendar of events, and this has significant advantages for the country. The most critical aspect remains that festivals should offer unique experiences.

About the Author: Professor Melville Saayman *is director of the research focus area TREES (Tourism Research in Economic Environs and Society) at North-West University (Potchefstroom Campus) in South Africa. He has served on numerous tourism related boards as a director, both locally and internationally.*

For more information visit
www.nwuexperts.co.za

2016
14 Amazing
FESTIVALS
in Africa

Here's Tourism Tattler's selection of amazing music and cultural festivals taking place in Africa during 2016 and should be in every tourists travel destination bucket list of unique experiences.

BOTSWANA

Dithubaruba Cultural Festival
03 September 2016

Hosted by Molepolole's Kgari Sechele Museum, this annual festival is commonly called *Kwa-ga-Mmakgosi* for its fun-filled days of diverse cultural festivities in music and dance, traditional *Bakwena* food varieties, attire and folk culture celebrations.

The Dithubaruba cultural festival demonstrates the lifestyles and customs of the traditional cultures of the Bakwena nation and it is used to promote and appreciate the diverse cultural practices in Kweneng District while also accommodating other ethnic groups, such as South Africa, to also share their culture. The festival is characterised by different genres of music, the commonly known *Setswana* music *dikhwaere* takes centre stage.

The Dithubaruba cultural festival is organised by the Botswana Tourism Board, the Botswana Ministry of Youth, Sports & Culture, and the Kgosi Sechele Museum.

For more information visit *www.botswanatourism.co.bw*

SOUTH AFRICA

AfrikaBurn
25 April - 01 May 2016

AfrikaBurn is the spectacular result of the creative expression of participants who gather once a year in the Tankwa Karoo region of the Western Cape, to create a temporary city of art, theme camps, costume, music and performance.

AfrikaBurn's aim is to be radically inclusive and accessible to anyone. The touchstone of value in this festival culture will always be immediacy: experience before theory, moral relationships before politics, survival before services, roles before jobs, ritual before symbolism, work before vested interest, participant support before sponsorship.

Nothing is for sale but ice at the event. Nothing. There are no vendors, no advertising or branding. It just doesn't fit in. It's not even a barter economy – it's a decommodified zone with a gift economy that's about giving without expecting anything in return.

For more information visit *www.afrikaburn.com/the-event/afrikaburn-2016*

ETHIOPIA

Timkat. Gondar
20 January 2016

Timkat, which means *baptism* in Amharic, is the Ethiopian Orthodox Tewahedo Church's celebration of Epiphany*, which represents the baptism of Jesus Christ in the Jordan River by John the Baptist. The Timkat celebration in Gondar is considered the most colourful, vibrant festival of the year.

While the Epiphany is celebrated all over the world, Timkat (also spelled Timket, or Timqat) is unique in its approach. On the eve of Timkat, the tabots, or sacred replicas of the Ark of the Covenant (containing the Ten Commandments), are wrapped in luxurious cloth and placed on the head of a priest to be carried out of the church in procession with the clergy. The pilgrimage ends just outside of the city at Fasilides' Bath, whereupon a Divine Liturgy is celebrated around 2am.

*[*Editor's Note: Epiphany celebrations vary. Eastern Orthodox Christians know the Epiphany as the baptism of Jesus Christ, whereas Western Christians celebrate the Epiphany as the recognition of the divinity of Christ by the Magi.]*

For more information visit *www.tourismethiopia.gov.et*

MALAWI

Chizangala – Gule wamkulu
June 2016

Also known as *'the Great Dance'*, Gule wamkulu is performed at the request of the village headman on the occasion of funerals of village members, puberty initiations, and the installation of chiefs and is part of the legacy of royal ritual inherited from the Chewa past. Gule wamkulu is today an essential feature of the Chewa countryside and has been recognized by UNESCO as a *Masterpiece of Intangible Heritage*. For more information visit www.visitmalawi.mw

MADAGASCAR

Madajazzcar
October 2016

The origins of the Festival International Madajazzcar dates back to October 1988, when a jazz club is created within the French Alliance of Tananarive (AFT), at the initiative of a trio of young jazz enthusiasts Malagasy doctors: Dr Allain Razakatiana Dr. Bruno and Dr. Henri Razafindrakoto Rakotondrabe. They were joined in 1989 by the late Dr. Hervé Razakaboana, who was also chairman of the jazz club AFT. The foundation of this jazz club AFT is the step that sealed the revival of jazz Malagasy, which already had decades of existence and creativity, contributing to one of Madagascar the first African country, with South Africa and Cameroon, to have a dynamic and talented musicians jazz scene.

For more information visit www.madajazzcar.mg

MOROCCO

Festival Mawazine Rythmes Du Monde
20 - 28 May 2016

The Mawazine Festival Rhythms of the World is held over nine days of free music without borders. The 12th edition of a festival attracted 2.5 million viewers of all ages, who came to celebrate the world's best artists and Morocco. The 2016 edition has an impressive line up of musicians already booked to perform.

For more information visit www.festivalmawazine.ma

MOZAMBIQUE

Umojafest
October 2016

"Umoja" is a Swahili word which means "unity", is the main theme of the festival. An artistic and cultural extravaganza that uniquely touches the spirit of the community, the Umoja Fest has historically been the most unifying celebration in the community, bringing people of all ethnic backgrounds together for a celebration of culture, education, social festivities and networking. Event highlights include the African Heritage Parade, Children's Day, African Drum & Dance, Jazz, Soul, Reggae, Spoken Word & Poetry, Hip-Hop Fest, Basketball Tournament, Fitness Demonstrations, Gospel Fest, Voter Registration, Vendor Marketplace & Community Resource Fair.

For more information visit www.visitmozambique.net

REUNION

SAKIFO Music Festival
3 - 5 June 2016

The 12th edition of the SAKIFO music festival takes place on the site of the White St Pierre Ravine in Reunion.

Since 2004, SAKIFO has provided music fans with everything they want, hence the name *Sakifo,* which means "enough" in the Reunion Creole language.

For more information visit *www.sakifo.com*

SEYCHELLES

Carnaval International de Victoria
22 - 24 April 2016

The 7th edition of the Seychelles International Carnival of Victoria will once again become a focal point for representatives from the world's most famous carnivals who have been invited to the islands to take part in this exciting international event.

The focus of international as well as local attention, the Seychelles International Carnival of Victoria features a procession of colourful floats representing the various participants' national carnivals, as well as a raft of other dedicated activities, all of which fall under the carnival's theme.

For more information visit *www.seychelles.travel*

SOUTH AFRICA

Oppikoppi Festival
07-09 August 2016

Founded in 1994, Oppikoppi (derived from the Afrikaans "op die koppie" or "on the hill") is South Africa's single largest music festival with attendance topping 20,000 revellers. The inaugural event primarily featured South African rock 'n' roll bands, and has since expanded to include a myriad of genres including hip hop, jazz, EDM, metal, soul, and kwaito – a purely South African spin on house music, remixing tribal rhythms to create the beats for inimitably danceable songs.

For more information visit *www.oppikoppi.co.za*

SWAZILAND

Marula Festival
February 2016

The Marula festival, known locally as *'Emaganwini'*, begins when the fruit is harvested by women and children in February. The ripe fruit is used to make Marula beer, the traditional toast of the festival. The royal family is the first to sample the brew and only after they take the first drink is the rest of the nation permitted to drink and celebrations begin. The largest single celebration is held at the royal residence of Ebuhleni, where the royal family join the nation in traditional song and dance..

For more information visit *www.thekingdomofswaziland.com*

TANZANIA, Zanzibar

Sauti za Busara Festival
9 - 12 February 2017

Dubbed as 'the Friendliest Festival on the Planet' the 13th edition of Sauti za Busara for 2016 has been cancelled after 13 years due to a shortage of funding. The organisers, Busara Promotions are urgently seeking partnerships with the public and private sectors to build a secure and sustainable future for the festival.

For more information visit *www.busaramusic.org*

UGANDA

Bayimba International Festival
September 2016

Kampala comes alive as a vibrant and eventful city when an unparalleled feast of music, dance, theatre, film, and visual arts from renowned and upcoming artists are staged for 9th edition of the Bayimba International Festival of the Arts.

For more information visit *www.bayimba.org/bayimba-festivals/bayimba-international-festival*

ZIMBABWE

Harare International Festival of the Arts **April - May 2016**

HIFA is a 6-day annual festival and workshop programme that showcases the very best of local, regional and international arts and culture in a comprehensive festival programme of theatre, dance, music, circus, street performance, spoken word, visual arts. HIFA has come to be seen as an important symbol of something positive about Zimbabwe, unifying socially and culturally disparate groups of Zimbabweans at a time of ideological conflict and political uncertainty bringing huge audiences together to celebrate something positive – the healing and constructive capacity of the arts.

For more information visit *www.hifa.co.zw*

Property Review

De Zeekoe Oudtshoorn

Farm Stays are growing in popularity and De Zeekoe in Oudtshoorn is more popular than most – and for good reason as it offers a truly unique South African farm experience to both domestic and international leisure travellers alike, writes **Des Langkilde**.

Having been referred to De Zeekoe for overnight accommodation by Cango Wildlife Ranch, where I had just completed a site inspection (read this review here), I arrived at the farm gate some seven kilometres outside of Oudtshoorn, in South Africa's Western Province with some trepidation. This is a working farm after all, and I'm used to the refined luxury of 5-star hotels and safari lodges.

My misgivings were soon dispelled however, when I checked-in at reception and met the guesthouse general manager, Kristy Potgieter who obliged me with a quick tour of the communal facilities.

When I visited in August 2015, the main entrance was being refurbished but judging by the decor and spotlighted cabinetry, displaying incredibly well crafted effigies of Meerkat among other ▶

tourist mementos, I was left with the impression of a boutique hotel rather than a farmstead establishment.

Moving from the reception area one enters the dining room, which is given a sense of ethereal spaciousness by virtue of open ceiling beams with simple unadorned square windows lining the space near the ceiling to provide more natural light. Sliding doors lead from the dining room to an open deck bar area, which overlooks a boma styled bonfire pit, a large swimming pool surrounded by expansive lawns, and views of the Olifants river, karoo veld and the spectacular Swartberg and Outeniqua mountains beyond.

The farm I am told is owner managed and covers an expanse of 2000 hectares, parts of which are cultivated for growing its main crop, alfalfa, which is supplied to the surrounding cattle farmers as feed. The farm was originally named 'Zeekoegat' over a century ago, which is a Dutch word meaning "hippo waterhole" referring to the abundance of hippo pods that used to frequent the riverbed that runs through the farm.

Concluding the tour I was shown to my room, which turned out to be one of two honeymoon bedrooms with balconies that overlook

the reed choked riverbeds below. The room is large enough to swing an ostrich without touching sides, and the mosquito net draped four-poster bed is expansive enough to share it with a dizzy ostrich too. The en-suite bathroom is also uncommonly large, and features sandstone tiles with a free standing bath, double basins and large open air shower. A pair of warm bathrobes are provided and the bath towels are luxuriously soft and absorbent. The room is tastefully decorated with ostrich feather cushions, persian carpets, soft lighting and complimentary sherry. As August in the karoo can be chilly, I was grateful to note the fireplace, which is lit by the bed turndown service while guests are at dinner. In addition to the two honeymoon suites, five superior, nine luxury and three standard bedroom options are offered at the main farm, and all have wheelchair-friendly access.

But that's not all - the farm also boasts four rustic self-catering cabins positioned on the banks of a picturesque lake. The lake is a short drive from the main farm lodging, but being early afternoon I decided to walk the five kilometres to take in the farms ambiance and crisp country air.

Activities on the farm are plentiful, as evidenced by a well maintained rack of mountain bikes for hire and a sign that I spotted on my walk that denotes self guided hiking trails of five and ten kilometre distances, cycling routes of fifteen to thirty kilometres, swimming, canoeing, fishing and bird spotting. Regarding the latter, the farm has recorded over 162 bird species, the most impressive of which are a mating pair of fish eagles whose distinctive call can be heard at regular intervals.

Having built up an appetite, I looked forward to sampling De Zeekoe's cuisine, the ingredients for which are harvested from the farms organic vegetable and herb garden. They even grow and press their own olive oil, and source their free-range beef, lamb and ostrich locally. The a la carte menu is impressive with choices ranging from beef, ostrich, or venison to vegetarian dishes. I started with a creamy butternut soup followed by a traditional Cape Malay Babotie served with couscous, chutney, deep fried onion rings, and small dumplings soaked in a spicy sauce - absolutely delicious and artfully presented. For dessert I opted for a simple steamed pudding with hot custard. My meal was complimented a glass of Merlot selected from the restaurants comprehensive wine list and cellar.

After a sherry nightcap and cigar enjoyed on my rooms balcony to the chorus of crickets and the rustle of mysterious wildlife foraging in the reeds below, I retired to a fitful sleep and arose before sunrise to depart for a Meerkat Adventure excursion - but that's another story that can be read on page 13.

Overall, De Zeekoe has set the bar for farm stay experiences that others will find hard to emulate.

For more information visit www.dezeekoe.co.za

City Lodge Group Opens Its First Downtown Johannesburg Hotel

The City Lodge Hotel Group has opened the first phase of rooms at its exciting 148-room City Lodge Hotel Newtown, Johannesburg with the hotel expected to be fully operational by the end of February.

The total development cost of the hotel is R146 million.

Situated in the vibey area of Newtown on the western side of Johannesburg's bustling CBD, City Lodge Hotel Newtown comprises seven storeys and includes two boardrooms (a 16-seater and a 10-seater), a mini-gym, a swimming pool, a coffee shop and a bistro-style lounge.

The new hotel, which takes the group's total number of hotels to 57, is ideally located adjacent to the Newtown Junction shopping centre and the African Museum and within easy reach of attractions such as the SAB World of Beer and the Market Theatre.

Positioned on the corner of Miriam Makeba and Carr streets, the hotel offers easy access to the CBD and the freeway system linking the city to other parts of Gauteng province. It is within easy reach of the Gautrain's Park Station which has links to Rosebank, Sandton, Midrand, Centurion, Pretoria and O R Tambo International Airport.

The hotel's general manager is Anton Rademeyer, who was previously the GM at Town Lodge Grayston Drive, Sandton. He has come up through the ranks within the group over the past 15 years and has a wealth of knowledge of the hotel industry.

Aimed at business travellers and leisure guests

While the hotel is aimed mainly at business travellers, it is bound to also attract leisure guests who visit the Newtown precinct for shows and the other art, culture and entertainment attractions the area has to offer. Other attractions in close proximity are the University of the Witwatersrand, the University of Johannesburg the weekend Neighbourgood's Market. The hotel is on the hop-on-hop-off open top Red Bus route.

Significantly, this is the first hotel that the City Lodge Hotel Group has developed in downtown Johannesburg. It ideally complements the group's other Johannesburg hotels situated in Rosebank, Sandton, Bryanston, Fourways, Randburg, Rivonia, Eastgate, Southgate, Roodepoort, Germiston, Brakpan, Isando and at OR Tambo International Airport.

"We are very excited about the prospects for City Lodge Hotel Newtown and believe that it will bring a vibrant new hotel product offering into downtown Johannesburg and look forward to it making a meaningful contribution to our group," said Clifford Ross, the City Lodge Hotel Group's chief executive.

The opening of City Lodge Hotel Newtown comes shortly after the opening of the 90-room Road Lodge Pietermaritzburg in December, 2015.

The City Lodge Hotel Group has 54 hotels in South Africa, two in Kenya and one in Botswana and is progressing with plans to open a further hotel in Kenya, and hotels in Tanzania, Mozambique and Namibia.

For more information visit www.clhg.com

City Lodge Hotel Newtown: Aimed at business travellers and leisure guests.

Legal

FROM THE
BENCH™
With Louis the Lawyer
BENCHMARK ©

CPA:
The Consumer Protection Act

- Part 1 -
CANCELLATION, PENALTIES & NON-REFUNDABLE DEPOSITS

NOTE: The Risk in Tourism series (The Law: Contracts) will continue with Part 18 in a future edition.

This is most probably the application of the CPA that has most often 'reared its head' in the travel and tourism industry – various sections of the CPA applies so let's look at each of them and then provide you with an executive summary:

THE COMMON LAW

This document suggests that the CPA has not revoked the common law per se. Thus such common law duties as *caveat emptor* and *caveat subscriptor*, especially read with my first point above, are in my view 'alive and well'.

Section 2 (10): Interpretation – also states that:
'No provision of this Act must be interpreted so as to preclude a consumer from exercising any rights afforded in terms of the common law'

Section 4 (2): Consumer Rights states that *'The court must develop the common law as necessary to improve the realisation and enjoyment of consumer rights generally, and in particular by persons contemplated in section 3(1)(b)'* (SEE BELOW)

Section 56 (4): Implied Warranty specifically states that the implied warrant contained in section 56 (1): *'... applies in addition to any other implied warranty or condition imposed by the common law'*.

The above may be read to imply that whilst consumer common law rights are retained and in fact enhanced, supplier common law rights have been revoked – I don't believe that to be the correct reading or implication of the CPA as inter alia the rules of interpretation clearly states that such a meaning must be unequivocal, which I do not believe to be the case.

SECTION 3: PURPOSE & POLICY

This section strengthens my argument above, namely in the choice of words addressing consumer behaviour:
- 'encouraging responsible and informed consumer choice and behaviour' [Section 3 (1)(e)]:
- 'the development of a culture of consumer responsibility' [Section 3 (1)(f)]:

It means in my view that a consumer cannot act recklessly and without due regard (i.e. irresponsibly) to common law principles (see previous paragraph) and then 'rely on/call upon' the CPA to 'rescue' him/her. However care should be taken by the supplier when dealing with consumers that fall into the following categories [Section 3 (1) (b)]:

- low-income persons or persons comprising low-income communities;
- live in remote, isolated or low-density population areas or communities;
- seniors or other similarly vulnerable consumers;
- whose ability to read and comprehend any advertisement, agreement, mark, instruction, label, warning, notice or other visual representation is limited by reason of low literacy, vision impairment or limited fluency in the language in which the representation is produced, published or presented [Read with Section 40 (2) Re 'Unconscionable Conduct'].

SECTION 4: REALIZATION OF CONSUMER RIGHTS

See in the two previous paragraphs the duty placed on the supplier vis a vis consumers that fall into the section 3 (1) (b) categories.

Section 4 (3) & (4) in addition directs any 'Tribunal or Court' to adopt the following approach when assessing documents that govern the relationship between the consumer & the supplier – it is VERY onerous for suppliers & must be borne in mind when not only drafting documents (e.g. T&C) but when engaging in the sales process (i.e. 'circumstances of the transaction'):

Section 4 (3): If any provision of this Act, read in its context, can reasonably be construed to have more than one meaning, the Tribunal or court must prefer the meaning that best promotes the spirit and purposes of this Act, and will best improve the realisation and enjoyment of consumer rights generally.

Section 4 (4): the Tribunal or court must interpret any standard form, contract or other document prepared or published by or on behalf of a supplier, or required by this Act to be produced by a supplier, to the benefit of the consumer—
- (a) so that any ambiguity that allows for more than one reasonable interpretation of a part of such a document is resolved to the benefit of the consumer; and
- (b) so that any restriction, limitation, exclusion or deprivation of a consumer's legal rights set out in such a document or notice is limited to the extent that a reasonable person would ordinarily contemplate or expect, having regard to—
- (i) the content of the document;
- (ii) the manner and form in which the document was prepared and presented; and
- (iii) the circumstances of the transaction or agreement.

To be continued in the March edition.

Understanding Tourism Trade Insurance
- Part 2 -

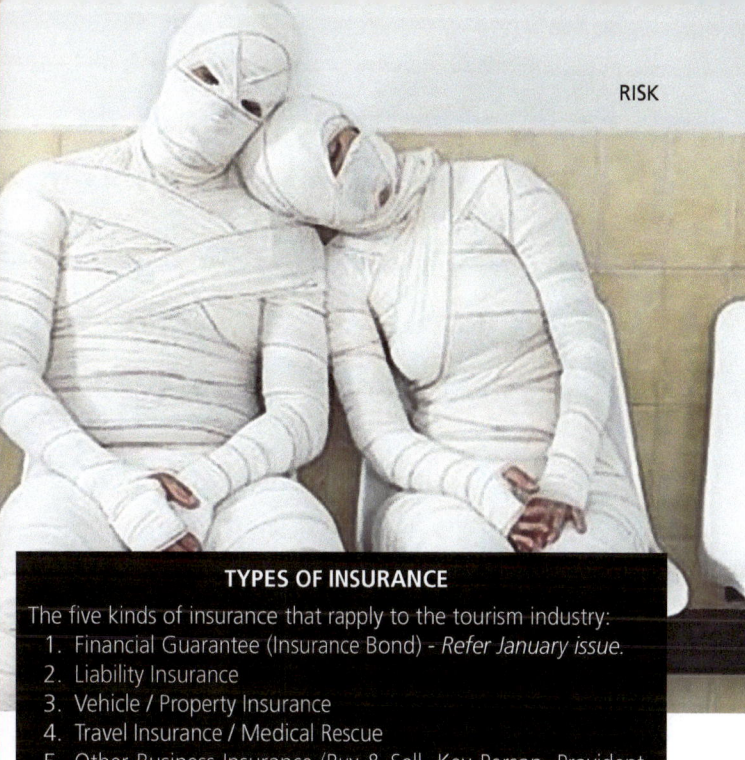

Part 1 in this series covered an introduction to insurance, an outline on the EC Directive and the basics of risk management, and the first of 5 important types of insurance, namely financial guarantees. In Part 2, we look at liability insurance, writes **Des Langkilde**.

TYPES OF INSURANCE

The five kinds of insurance that rapply to the tourism industry:
1. Financial Guarantee (Insurance Bond) - *Refer January issue.*
2. Liability Insurance
3. Vehicle / Property Insurance
4. Travel Insurance / Medical Rescue
5. Other Business Insurance (Buy & Sell, Key Person, Provident Fund)

---

2. Liability Insurance - what is it?

Liability insurance is a product that is bought by organisations, companies and individuals to cover the risk of a common law claim for damages by someone who is injured or suffers some form of quantifiable or financial loss through their activities whilst in the insured's care.

An added risk is the responsibility of maintaining private roads where a client may have an accident due to poor maintenance or an unmarked hazard or danger. Even secondary provincial roads that are in a poor state can become an issue and where this is the case you should continually lobby the local authority to rectify such, so as to emphasise their liability in this regard.

In South Africa, the SA National Road Traffic Act 93 of 1996 defines a public road as; *any road, street or thoroughfare or any other place (whether a thoroughfare or not) which is commonly used by the public or any section thereof or to which the public or any section thereof has a right of access, and includes;*
(a) *The verge of any such road, street or thoroughfare;*
(b) *Any bridge, ferry or drift traversed by any such road, street or thoroughfare; and*
(c) *Any other work or object forming part of or connected with or belonging to such road, street or thoroughfare.*

Legal opinion: By definition, a public road is not linked to the ownership of the road but to the common right of use to the road. A road may be considered private for purposes of road maintenance but if it used by the public, it is considered a public road in terms of the National Road Traffic Act, 1996. In terms of the law, very few roads are considered to be private as it would need to be proven that the road has access control and that no members of the public use the road at all.

Liability insurance covers your legal liability arising from accidents or other incidents which may occur at meetings, events, guided tours, safaris, transportation or simply on your premises where you are deemed to have been negligent. Examples include food poisoning, slipping on the floor, having an eye injured by the branch of a bush whilst on a game drive, being trampled by an elephant or even a bungi cord that breaks.

Negligence is simply doing something without a reasonable amount of care, or failing to have done something that might reasonably have been done to prevent the incident from having occurred in the first place.

NB: Most liability insurance policies only cover actions brought against the insured entity, unless the policy specifically extends to include 'all sub-contractors'. This is an important aspect, specifically from a Tour Operators' perspective, as they often sub-contract the services of Tourist Guides, for instance. Unless the policy wording is specifically extended, the Tourist Guides would need to have their own liability cover, which should be checked by the Tour Operator, for the reason that any actions instigated as a result of the Guide's negligence could result in the Tour Operator being found liable by virtue of contractual obligation. The same applies to Tour Brokers who sub-contract the services of Tour Operators.

TIP: As liability insurance is negligence based (fault must be proven in a court of law), it is important to ensure that the policy does not cap (limit) legal defence costs.

Why do you need it?

Some funding bodies, credibility associations such as SATSA and certain government regulations require that you have insurance cover in place before undertaking any tourism related activities. Without such cover, organisations are fully exposed to the risk of liability claims, which not only threatens their financial survival, their employees' jobs and the claimant's chances of being fully compensated but also impacts negatively on the general tourism industry and the destination country as a tourist destination. Here one must also consider that even if the action against the organisation is successfully defended in a court of law, the legal fees incurred over the lengthy process of defending the case can often exceed the amount of the initial demand. Again, most liability policies will cover the legal costs incurred in defending the case, but make sure that this cover is not limited to a level below the indemnity (sum insured) limit.

Understanding Tourism Trade Insurance - Part 2 (Continued)

What's available?

Liability policies come in several forms, two of these being: **General Public Liability** and **Passenger Liability** insurance. The reason that both covers are not offered in one policy is primarily due to the different risk profile or likelihood of occurrence to which insurance underwriters are exposed in each of the cover types.

A.I) GENERAL PUBLIC LIABILITY

General Public Liability insurance is designed specifically to protect you against any possible financial compensation claims by clients, guests or the general public where corporate or employee negligence could be construed to have been the cause of an incident. This covers a very broad variety of possible incidents ranging from loss or damage to a guest's personal property to a tourist claiming 'diminished value of holiday' due to their expectation of having a sea-facing room (as shown in the tour brochure) and ending up with a view of a brick wall.

How much cover is needed?

As a general rule it is far better to be *over* insured than *under* insured but this is directly proportionate to the affordability of the required premium. With insurance being perceived as a grudge purchase and the notion that "it will never happen to me" the temptation is to go for the cheapest cover but this can prove to be a false economy.

So how much is 'sufficient'? The required cover or indemnity limit could depend on the 'net worth' profile of your clients. For example, consider a 40-something, married South African business executive who earns ZAR500 000 a year, who is the sole breadwinner and has three dependents. He or she slips in the shower at your lodge and sustains a disabling injury to the spine and is unable to perform the same job as done before the incident. After a lengthy and costly legal case the court finds that you were negligent for not ensuring that the shower was fitted with non-slip tiles or mats. A possible award to the plaintiff could be in the region of ZAR10 million in this example, if one takes into account the costs of on-going medical care, loss of income and even alterations to the family home to make it wheelchair friendly.

Now consider the event of multiple claimants, or foreign guests whose income and future medical costs need to be calculated in their currency of origin. Quite obviously, the cover amount needed corresponds to the profile of guests that your establishment caters for.

Liability claims can be very high as they are rarely based on tangible factors, but on emotion and suffering, and therefore may be ridiculous and blown out of all proportion. However any such claim will be influenced by the following factors:

- Negligence has to be proven – was your company truly at fault? Are your floor tiles dangerous, do you have sufficient signage, was the ranger driving recklessly, was the guide qualified and taking reasonable care when he walked the group up to the elephant?
- Was the client made aware of any risk and did they sign an indemnity form? This will certainly relinquish some responsibility but not in the event of true negligence. Signage and information given either verbally or in writing to clients is imperative. This may often be in your marketing literature where the risks and shortcomings of a tour or experience must be clearly stated.
- How did you handle the situation after the event? Don't ever openly admit negligence such as, "sorry it was my / our fault." Handle the situation with compassion and understanding and where possible try and remedy the problem. Isolate the individual or people involved from your other guests and don't let anyone else who is not directly involved or who is not able to offer proper medical assistance anywhere near the clients or the incident. It is often others who encourage, incite and worsen an already difficult situation.
- Make sure that everything is accurately recorded and that comprehensive statements are taken from all relevant people. Sometimes photographs might help.
- Ensure that your company is fully compliant with all the local laws that govern your specific industry and all the staff that work for you. Health regulations must be met, guides must be licensed and qualified, buildings must meet certain standards, etc.
- Inquire as to what other insurance the client might have. Most people travel with their own insurances and in many cases, are covered for such eventualities. In fact, specifically for clients travelling on tours, it is advisable to make personal insurance compulsory. However, in the event of blatant negligence, the other insurance company would still try and recover from your insurance or look for recourse against you.
- If applicable, inform the booking agent that the client booked through of exactly what happened so that they are well informed. These incidents have a habit of mushrooming once an ill-informed agent gets involved. This is especially important in the case of an injury or death where next of kin must be notified.

TIP: Contracting a specialist, medical emergency response service is advisable as your liability for decisions made in a crisis situation will be transferred to the service provider and the incident recorded for future reference in the event of a personal injury claim being instituted against you. NB: Ensure that the service provider has sufficient medical malpractice insurance cover in place.

A well-operated business must try and be as professional as possible so as to avoid the risk of actions of this nature. However no matter how hard we try there is always a chance of the unlikely happening and of course some clients are specifically looking for this eventuality. As these claims are often made in foreign currency, cover needs to be fairly substantial, usually in tens of millions. However do not become neurotic! Do not succumb to the obvious person who is trying to ruin your business. Make sure that your house is in order and fight the

ridiculous claims and you should never have a problem. Remember that you are covered for those individuals who have a genuine claim.

Accidents will happen and it is comforting to know that your insurance will pay compensation to the unfortunate person who does lose an eye or damage their back by slipping. It must not be seen as losing a battle or admitting guilt but as a necessary backup for a genuine situation. Your insurance underwriter will fight for you. The problem may arise when you are not sufficiently covered for the magnitude of the claim. That is when your business is at risk because the shortfall would be payable by you, the service provider.

TIP: Any claim of this nature must be heard in a court within the country in which you do business. **Never** sign a contract that requires you to accept a foreign law as the presiding law and which might mean that you have to defend yourself in a foreign country or where you sign your rights away to a booking office where you acknowledge responsibility / liability for any accident / incident.

AII) PASSENGER LIABILITY

This covers incidents resulting from the transportation of passengers by land, sea or air and can often be included as part of a Motor, Marine or Aviation insurance policy.

TIP: Care must be taken to check that the motor policy wording does not exclude fare-paying passengers.

It is unlikely that an underwriter will be prepared to cancel or amend the wording of a standard motor vehicle policy, so make sure that the cover obtained is specifically for fare-paying passenger liability. These policies will invariably contain clauses in the policy wording that oblige you to comply with certain regulatory conditions, such as those in South Africa, which are laid down by the Department of Transport (Tour Operators Permit, Drivers' PRDP, etc). In addition there may be certain mechanical devices required such as seat belts or speed inhibitors.

Passenger liability insurance basically covers passengers while in transit in a specified vehicle in the event of an accident. This is therefore an essential form of insurance and one that is most likely to be called upon. Many basic comprehensive vehicle policies carry a certain amount of passenger liability insurance but this is generally insufficient and does not cover all eventualities and geographical regions. It is therefore imperative that this section of a vehicle policy is beefed up and it is up to the individual company to make sure that all the regions in which they operate are covered by their policy.

To obtain a transport permit for a passenger-carrying vehicle, the law in South Africa currently stipulates a minimum of ZAR5 million per seven passengers on board and proof of such cover is required before a permit will be issued. This is generally sufficient but once again the individual company must assess their particular risk. Fortunately this insurance is not prohibitively expensive although one might have to find a broker with specific experience in this field to assist you in finding the appropriate cover.

*This article, to be continued in the February 2013 edition of the Tourism Tattler, will elaborate on Passenger Liability insurance and cover the impact that the Road Accident Fund Amendment Bill in South Africa has had on this class of insurance cover - **Ed**.*

Mercedes Sprinter Sets the Standard

The success story of Mercedes-Benz Sprinter vans is difficult to beat, especially considering that more than 25 000 Sprinters have been sold to South African customers since the year 2000.

One should always be cautious in using superlatives. Nevertheless, the success story that began on that momentous day is one that would tempt even the most down-to-earth of us to wax lyrical. Indeed, this is the day that can confidently be described as marking the dawn of a new era for the van sector.

The large van caused quite a sensation at the time: among one of its highlights, it was the first van to be fitted as standard with disc brakes on both front and rear wheels, as well as with the ABS anti-lock braking system. The international motoring media were so impressed they voted the Sprinter the "Van of the Year 1995".

Two decades later and the Sprinter is still a true pioneer, having defined an entire segment, to which it has even given its name.

Whenever the automotive press talk about the major players in the world of vans, it's often referred to in terms of the "Sprinter class".

"Only the Mercedes-Benz Sprinter can offer unmatched reliability, perfect driving features and an innate ability to reinvent itself over such a long period of time. This is a vehicle that prides itself on being everything to everyone who purchases it: exceptional safety, impressively low fuel consumption, reliability and a widely-respected high resale value. These are just some of the key factors that contribute to the Sprinter being the most dominant player in the segment," says Nicolette Lambrechts, Vice-President: Mercedes-Benz Vans.

"What is even more exciting than celebrating such a significant

milestone is the fact that the Sprinter not only has two decades of experience to tap into, but also the idea of the current and future Sprinter exemplifying impeccable workmanship, build quality of the highest standard and endless innovation," added Lambrechts.

The year 2013 saw the arrival of the latest Sprinter in the market – a vehicle with which Mercedes-Benz Vans is once again setting new standards in terms of safety and economy. In November 2014, just a year after its introduction worldwide, the 222,222nd new Sprinter was delivered into customer hands.

Although its appearance has changed over the years, the secret of the Sprinter family's success has stayed the same.

The new Sprinter impresses with innovations in the fields of safety and economy.

It is the first van in its class to be made available with engines that meet the Euro VI emissions standard, proving that even the big boys on the road can be environmentally friendly and economical. Despite the engines on offer in South Africa adhering to Euro V emissions standards - due to the unavailability of appropriate fuel - the Sprinter still boasts operating the cleanest engine in the large van segment.

But it is not just thanks to its frugal fuel consumption that the new van is top of the class in the large vans segment, which the vehicle's distant ancestor once defined as the "Sprinter class".

It also sets standards with respect to safety, loaded with various assistance systems such as COLLISION PREVENTION ASSIST, Blind Spot Assist and Lane Keeping Assist.

For more information visit www.mercedes-benz.co.za